Start-Up
Connections
ELECTRICITY

Stewart Ross

Evans

Evans Brothers Limited

First published in this edition in 2010

Published by Evans Brothers Limited
2A Portman Mansions
Chiltern Street
London W1U 6NR

Produced for Evans Brothers Limited by
White-Thomson Publishing Ltd.,
+44 (0) 843 2087 460
www.wtpub.co.uk

Printed & bound in China by New Era Printing
Company Limited

Editor: Dereen Taylor
Consultants: Nina Siddall, Head of Primary School
Improvement, East Sussex; Norah Granger, former
primary head teacher and senior lecturer in Education,
University of Brighton; Kate Ruttle, freelance literacy
consultant and Literacy Co-ordinator, Special Needs
Co-ordinator, and Deputy Headteacher at a primary
school in Suffolk.
Designer: Leishman Design
Cover design: Balley Design Limited

British Library Cataloguing in Publication Data
Llewellyn, Claire
      Electricity. -- (Start-up connections)
      1. Electricity--Juvenile literature.
      I. Title II. Series
      537-dc22

ISBN: 978 0 237 54171 2

Acknowledgements:
Special thanks to the following for their help and
involvement in the preparation of this book: Staff and
pupils at Elm Grove Primary School, Brighton, Liz
Price and family and friends.

Picture Acknowledgements:
Liz Price 20, 21.
Mary Evans Picture Library 9.
All other photographs by Chris Fairclough.

Contents

Electricity in school

It's a busy day at school. Everyone has machines to help them do their work. These machines all run on electricity.

Jane is working at the computer.

The head teacher is talking on the telephone.

machines electricity computer

Ernest is doing sums using his calculator.

The cook is taking food out of the freezer.

telephone calculator freezer

Electrical appliances

Many things run on electricity.
They are called electrical appliances.

▼ Look at the things in this picture.

Which of them are electrical appliances?
Which of them are not?

electrical appliances   lights   printer

George made a list of the electrical appliances in school.
He went into a classroom, the office, the kitchen
and the hall.

Classroom	Office	Kitchen	Hall
lights	lights	lights	lights
computer	computer	fridge	heater
printer	telephone	freezer	
tape recorder	printer	kettle	
clock	fax machine	mixer	
	photocopier		
	clock		
	calculator		

Which room has the most appliances?
Make a list of the appliances in your kitchen at home.

photocopier   mixer   heater

What does it do?

Some electrical appliances give out light, like a torch. Some give out heat, like a fire. Some make sounds, like a tape recorder. Some have moving parts, like a washing machine.

▶ Match each of these electrical appliances with the words below.

light heat sound moving parts

light heat sounds

In the past, before there was electricity, people used different kinds of appliances in their homes.

How did people light their homes?

► This is how people made toast, one hundred years ago.

Mains electricity

◀ Jake's dad is cleaning the carpet. He plugs the vacuum cleaner into a socket in the wall. Then he switches it on.

▲ When we plug electrical appliances into a socket, they use electricity from the mains. Electricity flows along the flex and into the machine.

socket   switches on   plug

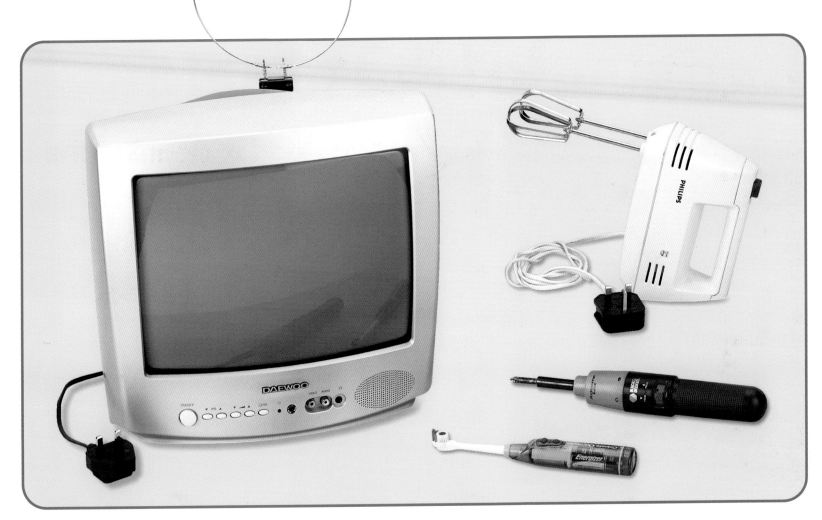

▲ Look at these appliances. Which ones use electricity from the mains?

How can you tell?

mains flows flex dangerous **11**

Looking at batteries

Alex's remote control car does not run on mains electricity. It runs on batteries instead. Batteries store electricity.

◀ The remote control handset also runs on batteries. Alex needs to fit a new battery. Can you see the right way to put it in?

batteries   store

Small batteries store a little electricity. Big batteries store much more. Look at the objects in the pictures.

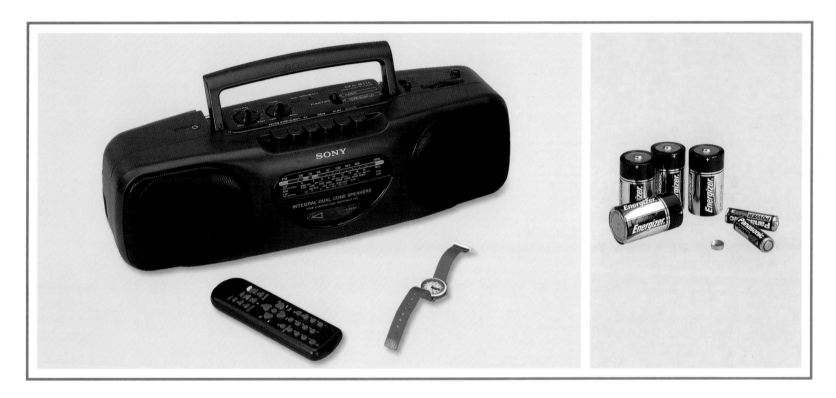

Can you match each appliance to the right batteries?

What other things use batteries?

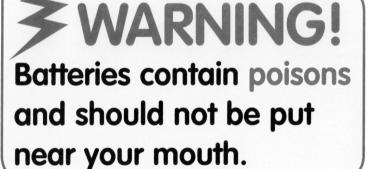

WARNING!

Batteries contain poisons and should not be put near your mouth.

Lights and light bulbs

▶ **When Olivia's mum switches on the lamp, the light bulb lights up.**

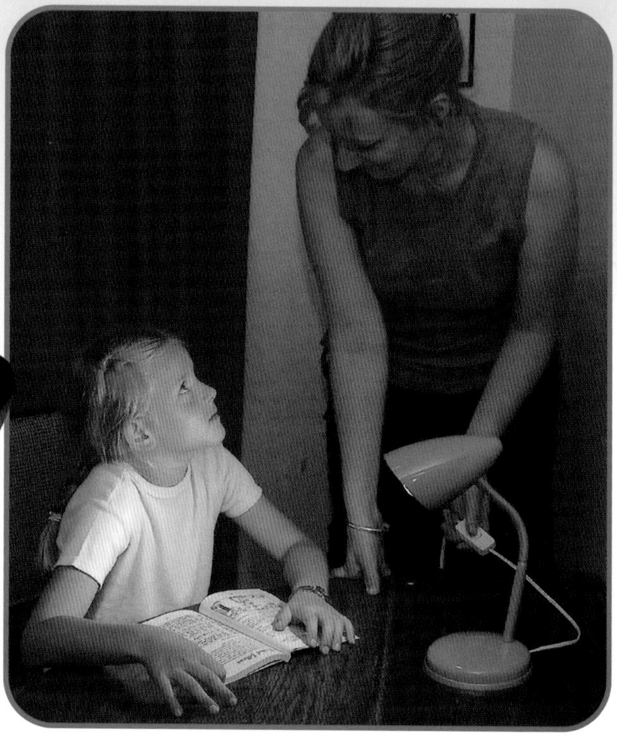

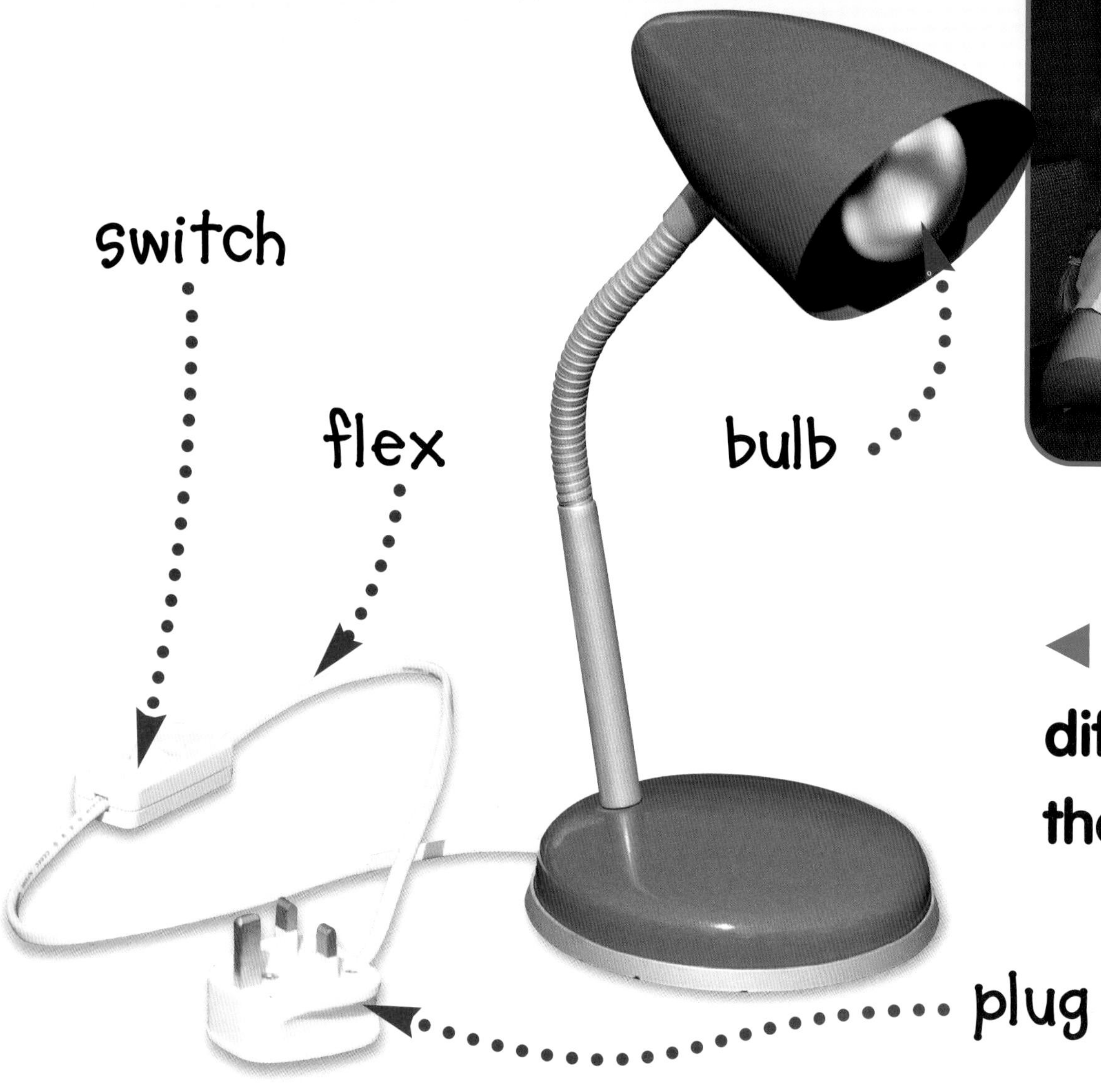

switch

flex

bulb

◀ **Look at the different parts of the lamp.**

plug

lamp   light bulb

Look closely at another light bulb. Inside, you can see a metal wire called a filament. This is the part that shines brightly when you switch the light on.

filament .....

WARNING!
Never touch electrical switches or plugs when you have wet hands. Water and electricity together are very dangerous.

Light up a bulb

Owen is going to make his own light. His teacher has given him everything he needs.

 crocodile clips and plastic-coated wire

 bulb

batteries

To get electricity from the battery to the bulb, Owen needs to give it a pathway. This pathway is called a circuit.

▶ First Owen screws the bulb into the bulb holder.

pathway circuit bulb holder

▼ **Then he connects the wires to the batteries using the crocodile clips.**

▼ **Finally he connects the wires to the bulb holder.**

Hooray! The bulb lights up!

connects crocodile clips

What went wrong?

Harry and Mary cannot make their bulbs light up. There is a problem with their circuits.

▼ Can you see how Harry can fix his circuit?

▼ **There is a different problem with Mary's circuit. Can you see what it is?**

How a circuit works

▼ These children are acting out the circuit to show how it works. When the children hold hands D's bulb lights up.

This shows how electricity flows around a circuit.

▼ **When two children drop hands, D's bulb goes out.**

Electricity cannot flow because the circuit is broken.

A = battery   B and C = crocodile clips and
plastic-coated wire   D = bulb holder with bulb

broken

Further information for Parents and Teachers

ELECTRICITY ACTIVITY PAGE

Use the activities on these pages to help you to make the most of Electricity in your classroom.

Activities suggested on this page support progression in learning by consolidating and developing ideas from the book and helping the children to link the new concepts with their own experiences. Making these links is crucial in helping young children to engage with learning and to become lifelong learners.

Ideas on the next page develop essential skills for learning by suggesting ways of making links across the curriculum and in particular to science, numeracy and ICT.

WORD PANEL

Check that the children know the meaning of each of these words from the book.

appliance	filament	mains
batteries	flex	movement
bulb holder	flow	plug
circuit	heat	sound
connect	light	switch
crocodile clip	light bulb	wire

SAFETY FIRST

What do the children already know about safety and electricity?
- Use pages 10 -11 of the book as a basis for discussion.
- Together, make a class list of ways of keeping safe and things that are not safe to do.
- Ask children to make posters or lists of rules for safe use of electricity. Encourage the children to take their work home so that the message can continue to be reinforced there.

POWER SURVEY

Groups of children can visit different parts of the school, looking for ways in which electricity is used. Remind them to look at both mains and battery appliances.
- Ask children to write or draw each different example of ways in which electricity is used.
- Teach them to use a tally system so that they can record quantity

- Use a plan of the school and record the number of uses in each area of the school.
- Ask children to try to explain why different parts of the school have different requirements. For example:
  - Which parts of the school are best lit? Why?
  - Do offices or classrooms need more appliances?
  - Do classrooms for younger children have more than those for older children? Why?
  - Where are most battery-driven appliances used? Why?

SAVING POWER

Once they have completed a power survey, tell the children that you'd like them to think of ways of using electricity sensibly so that it's not wasted.
- If appropriate, link to money and talk about what the school could buy if it saved money on bills.
- Talk about the reasons you found for using electricity and clarify that the idea isn't to stop using electricity, but to use it sensibly and save waste.
- Show children the 'stand-by' lights on appliances so that they know that the appliances are still using electricity. Explain why it's good to turn 'stand-by' off if the appliance will be unused for a while.

SUSTAINABLE ELECTRICITY

Establish what children already know about sustainable power. Are there any landmarks in your local area which you could visit or refer to? E.g. a wind turbine, a wind farm, a building with solar panels, an eco-house or even a power station?

If not, find pictures of different forms of power generation online as prompts for discussion.
- Give children the chance to use a wind-up radio or a dynamo-torch. Compare with using a battery-powered radio or torch.
- Which is easier to use? What are the advantages of using each type of torch?
- Show children the solar cell on a calculator. Talk about how bigger solar panels can be used to save electricity in houses.
- Once you have explored a variety of ways of making electricity, ask groups of children to co-operate to make collages of houses which use as little electricity as possible - and only for the most important things.

USING ELECTRICITY FOR CROSS CURRICULAR WORK

The revised national curriculum focuses on children developing key competencies as

- successful learners
- confident individuals and
- responsible citizens.

Cross curricular work is particularly beneficial in developing the thinking and learning skills that contribute to building these competencies because it encourages children to make links, to transfer learning skills and to apply knowledge from one context to another. As importantly, cross curricular work can help children to understand how school work links to their daily lives. For many children, this is a key motivation in becoming a learner.

The web below indicates some areas for cross curricular study. Others may well come from your own class's engagement with the ideas in the book.

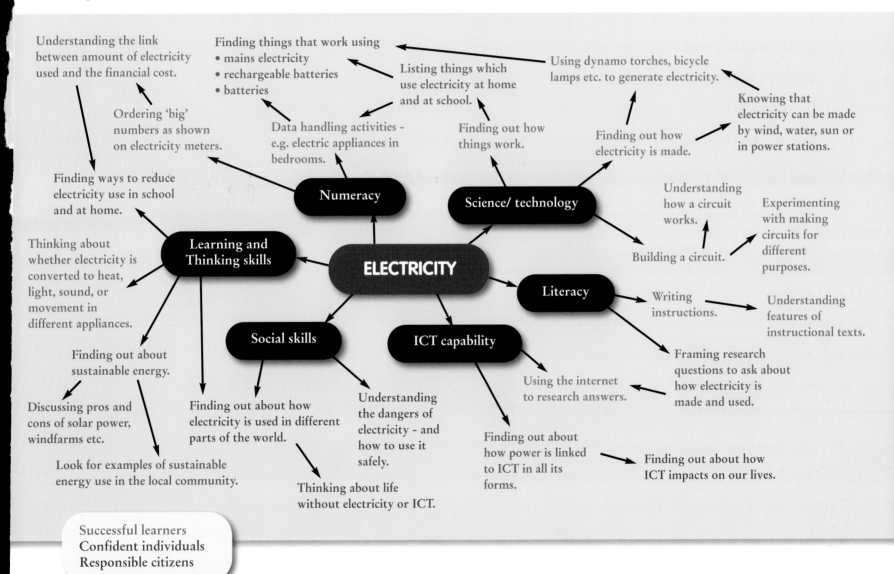

Index